my
skin
looks
after
me

BY JANE BUXTON

ILLUSTRATED BY JENNIFER COOPER

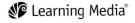 Learning Media®

Granddad and I
like to go exploring.

Look!
Here's a
lizard's
skin!

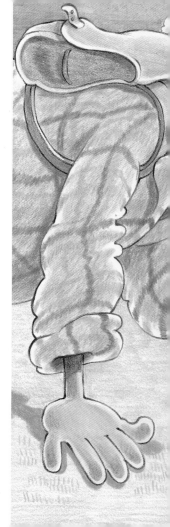

My skin is growing all the time.
I lose bits of old skin all
the time, too.

My skin sweats to help me cool down when I'm hot.

Sometimes, I scrape some skin off.

6

My skin is good at keeping dirt out.

My skin is good at keeping
water out, too.

9

I keep my skin clean.
I eat food that is good for it.

I look after my skin,
and my skin looks after me.